The

MILLIONAIRE
MARKETER

in

ASSISTED
LIVING

*How to attract legions of residents and get
talented staff into your homes*

R. CAMPER BULL

Dedication

This book is dedicated to Gene Guarino, who has taught so many, including us here at Heightener, how to truly do good by doing well. His constant push to be a better version of himself has led to a great and thriving community that is embracing the opportunity in Residential Assisted Living to make their lives and the world a better place. It is our greatest pleasure to know him and be able to help you make positive impacts today.

Contents

Introduction

It is our responsibility to take care of the older generation. If you're reading this book with that sentiment in mind, you deserve to be thanked. You deserve to be recognized for the important work that you're doing to preserve one of the greatest generations; the generation that put us on this path and moved us forward. This is the generation that deserves all of the benefits that we can give them. So thank you for doing this and for helping them. Thank you for all of that from the bottom of my heart. It's important to recognize that we are doing something good here.

The reason I say this is because I've had the situation where my father, although still with it, needed some support, needed some help. He needed someone around. When we looked around, we did not find anyone. So at the age of 40, I went back and started living with my father. He was fine and it was a great blessing because I got the opportunity to spend his last years with him, learning from him, and being with him. In fact, once a week we'd go out and have lunch. I would ask him about his younger days and he'd regale me with anecdotes and stories from his past, and we'd share a good laugh together. However, I can tell you, on several occasions my father didn't understand what I did. He would barge into a conference call because he wanted to ask a question, not understanding that there were people from around the world talking to me. Nonetheless, this was precious time, time I feel fortunate to have spent with him, despite the many challenges.

This is clearly a very important project for me. It helps me make sure that the generation that has paved our way, paved my work and your work, is taken care of. So thank you.

Moore's Law

By the time you finish reading this book, something is going to be out of date! According to Gordon Moore, one of the founders of Intel, "The number of transistors and resistors on a chip doubles every 18 months". In a time frame of 18 to 24 months, the entire industry hardware changes and that's the slowest part! The software changes even faster! Case in point: Google's rating and ranking system changes almost every day!

So this book is designed to give you broad outlines, not specific tactics. These broad outlines have worked for years and will continue to work because they are fundamental to the business of the Internet. We will not be giving you specific things, specific pointers, because by the time this book is printed and put in your hands, things will have changed!

Moore's law has been and continues to be consistent for over 50 years now. We continue to learn and grow, but this is a book designed to help get you started and move you in the right direction. The rules we create and the takeaways of this book will remain consistent as well. The URLs (Uniform Resource Locators) may change and the current social media darlings will be replaced with others. The pundits will have their ideas, however this does not detract from the fact that these are fundamental marketing procedures used on the Internet; tried and tested over the last 10 years. Will they stand the test of time? Yes. Will the URLs and how we execute these, change? Absolutely. Understand that this is designed to get you going. Most of what happens on the Internet is similar if you use the standard rules. The specifics will always change. The rules continue to be the same.

The Land Grab

When the West was being settled, one of the things that we found was that a family could go out into the west, get to a certain place, and claim land. On April 22, 1889, some 50,000 people came together at midday to stake claim to 2 million acres of land. People were allowed to claim up to 160 acres each. As long as they lived on it and worked on it, they would receive the title to that piece of land. There was literally a run to grab a piece of land. Many such land runs were organized all the way until 1901.

People would claim land by simply running from a start point and grabbing a piece of land that they would then nurture into a real farm. There were two ways to do this: One way was to get on a fast horse and grab something and then have the rest of the family follow. The other way to do this was to have the whole family slowly trudge in and see what they could find. They both worked.

It was interesting that during the first land grab, people who ran fast to grab it, may have grabbed what they thought was the best land and the most prime real estate. However, since there was so much land around, the covered wagons that went beyond, found other land to claim and benefited just as much as the fast horses.

In both instances, it worked out just as well and the people managed to create successful holdings in both cases. I believe that the families that came in later were the ones that slowly helped create interconnected communities. They offered support and helped families and holdings survive difficult times.

There is a modern parallel here: we are in a land grab right now; and this follows three stages. The Internet is not new to us, but think about how it was during its infancy: the first land grab was by people trying to grab the best and the brightest areas on the Internet. These were the areas that they were going to make money on by reselling. Then came the actual development of websites. This was the tough part. People had to learn coding, processes and programming. It is both difficult and time consuming to learn this. The Internet was slow and access to it was limited. Dial up connections were slow, tedious and limiting.

Taking a look at right now, the Internet is fast and ubiquitous. However, the first ship has sailed. All of the great URLs have been purchased and are being sold for tens or hundreds of thousands of dollars. There are speculators holding tens of thousands of URLs, hoping someone's going to pay for them; great big programs are being created, dealt with, and being speculated on. We now have single-window clearances for most solutions that we need. For instance, Google takes over and is able to provide you instant information in the local area and pretty much all the other information you need.

The opportunity for land grab still exists. This is the third stage and there is an abundance of local information that is still unavailable. There is still a lot of untapped potential. The opportunity to create local communities on the Internet still holds great value, not only to the people on it, but to the Internet itself. In that way, now is the best time to really step up and create a place both physically as well as virtually for your home and your organization. There is no better time than now as the third set of land grab starts, and we start to really focus on the local geographic area and how we can best leverage the process.

Get Online and Be Consistent

Given the expansive nature and the hypervelocity of the growth of the Internet and the World Wide Web, perspective is still important. Consider the fact that in 1992, there were 10 websites on the World Wide Web; by 2016 there were 1 billion! This was a massive expansion over 25 years and it completely changed the way we see the world. There were substantial growth opportunities from 1991 to 2010, but things really took off between 2010 and 2015 when we saw a massive increase. From 2016 to 2017, there was a massive 69% increase to one 1.7 billion websites! This was an unprecedented number that was expanding every day! In 2018, we will approach 2 billion websites. So it took 25 years to get the first billion websites and it took two years to get the second billion! That's some perspective for you!

The growth of the Internet is unprecedented in human history. Examine our ability to distribute information - from the time of the Gutenberg Bible when the advent of the printed book in the West enabled publications to be widely distributed, to the present time when the Internet potentially gives access to everyone in the world almost immediately! This has changed the world, the way we think, the way we market, and the way we live.

It is not just high tech companies that are online. It is not just for the glitterati and the social media mavens. An online presence is now a sort of prerequisite for our very existence. If you're not online, you do not exist internationally, nationally, or even locally! It's becoming more and more ubiquitous to use the Internet for practically anything: to search for people, get information, medical advice, locate places, read history, get the news, find out about the latest research, get relationship advice... you name it!

Therefore it is important that houses create and develop their own site, which people can research, locate and find out more about. Residential Assisted Living houses have the same advantage of the Internet other people have; an advantage that can really make a huge difference. If this advantage is not exploited by you, it will be by someone else!

As everyone is aware, the key to a web presence is an actual URL (Uniform Resource Locator). This is your online address, just like you have an address for your home. Today it is as important to have an Internet address if not more so! Having an address on the World Wide Web is vital, because people are looking and searching for you on the net and you have to make it easy for them to find you. It is important to capture your online presence now, because going forward, it will become more and more difficult to find and get URLs that are appropriate, specific and useful in marketing and advertising your Residential Assisted Living house. This is no longer optional; it isn't just something that would be nice to have. An online presence is an absolute necessity; more so now than ever before as more people capture those addresses and hoard them. There are people who are hoarding addresses and charging $5,000, $50,000 or $100,000 dollars for a simple URL address because they recognize the power of that address. Therefore, every house should have a dedicated website for itself.

When people are looking for a place to put their parents, their mother and father, they're not looking for a long menu. They're looking for a specific area, a specific house, and therefore each one of your houses should absolutely have their own URL and live website specifically designed and captured as soon as possible; preferably something that is self-explanatory and easy to find employing Google's search algorithms. It is more and more important as the URLs disappear that we capture the ones that both, best speak to a customer and draw customers into your point of presence.

This is also important to help you create a lasting legacy in the online world. One of the things Google looks at very carefully is how long you've been online and how active you are on your web presence. Therefore, getting an appropriate URL is important not only because they're disappearing, but also because you want to start off your timer quickly… the timer showing your house as a valuable and active part of the World Wide Web, as well as the community of Residential Assisted Living.

Due to the unprecedented speed of development and the limitations of having a finite number of URLs to choose from, now is the best time to get involved, to make a stand, to put up your flag and claim your area in the virtual environment. So that when people are looking, they find you as an individual who's been there, is ranked well, and is both valued and understood.

Another reason why it is very important that we get on the Internet as quickly as possible: Google really rewards longevity. So, if you keep a URL active, interesting, and up to date long enough, Google will give that a higher ranking than someone new or stagnant. So getting on, even if you don't have a house right now, it is vitally important to actually use your name to stake your claim; to start building the edifice of an organization even before you have the actual house. This is necessary, because Google is interested in making sure that you are there, that you've been there for a while and that you're consistent. Create this as quickly as possible: capture that URL and own it and let Google start searching it on a regular basis to know that you're an active part of the Internet community.

Plus, you have to be consistent. Consistency becomes vitally important, because while to err is human, remember the Internet is not human! It looks to see if you are consistent across all areas based on certain formulae. For instance, Google likes and rewards 'Name, Address, Phone' or NAP consistency, which means that your business's name, address, and phone numbers match, wherever they are listed across the web. This is particularly important for local SEO (Search Engine Optimization).

If you are consistent, Google likes that better and continues to give you greater opportunities. If there are inconsistencies, if for instance the stated address varies, if the spelling of the name is not quite the same, if phone numbers change frequently, you get deranked. The search engine algorithm detects inconsistency and becomes confused. It is no longer certain that this is the same person or entity. It presumes that something is wrong.

The system doesn't know what is wrong and doesn't expect you to actually make errors about your own information. It expects to see uniformity and consistency; to have one source of data to be reinforced or corroborated by another. So when things are consistent and remain so, individuals and businesses become more accurately searchable, and detectable. What the Internet is looking for, what Google is looking for, is a long, broad consistency of information, not necessarily a specific area.

So, here are the takeaways: one house, one URL. Get it.

Secure the URL and get online because Google and the ranking systems reward a consistently visible presence. The legacy of your home is directly tied to its presence and legacy on the Internet. Short term players wait. Long term players get something up and move forward.

When considering a URL, the suffix is important. If you can obtain a ".com" address, this is best. The primary reason for this is that most people will type in the URL with .com. It is the most used one and the one people will presume to use before looking to use a .info or .org, or .net or even a country specific suffix. Going past that; some suffixes also have specific meanings. If you cannot find a ".com", work through that. Make your URL simple to use, simple to spell, and easy to type. It's okay if you capitalize things in the URL, but using symbols or dashes make it more difficult to explain and type. If you cannot find a ".com", a ".us", or ".co" would work better. When you start getting into the ".website" and other longer domain suffixes, it becomes more difficult to explain. Most people may not readily recognize those as website addresses yet, so steer clear of those as much as possible.

Here are some startling statistics to give you a clearer idea about the reach of the Internet:

- As of April 2018, the Internet Assigned Numbers Authority (IANA), an American body that supervises allocations of IP addresses worldwide among other things, recognized about 1543 top-level domains (or TLDs) in its official list! That's .com, .us, .net, .org, .edu and 1538 other such extensions for URLs.

- Do you know how many .com domains have been registered until August 2018? 137,096,963! The second most commonly used TLD is .tk — at a distant 21,148,627 domains.

- As of August 2018, the US hosts the highest number of IP addresses in the world, at a whopping 1,589,084,784.

What is the takeaway? Not having an online presence isn't an option anymore. The key is to find the URL that works best for you.

Be Where Your Customers Are Looking

With the additional one billion websites being created, there is a marked increase in the marketing and advertising of websites and products as well. However, the good news is that you have an advantage as an individual owning a Residential Assisted Living home. You have an advantage over most of the people building these websites now – the fact that you have a physical address! Google loves physical addresses, so utilize that. Take advantage of this fact, as well as the fact that since you have a physical address, people are going to be looking for you at that physical address.

You do not have to worry about advertising to the entire world. You have to worry about advertising to people in a specific area. I would suggest advertising between a 50 and 100 mile radius. My experience and available data suggests that most people don't want to have their parents outside of that radius. Even if they decide to move their parent(s) a little further away from where they live, they are unlikely to move them several hundred miles away from them. It is most likely that they would choose to have their parents live within an one or two hours commuting distance.

So you have a supreme advantage in creating a geographically specific informational site, and Google helps you do that almost immediately. The Internet likes the idea that they can point to an actual location; a non-Internet place and say, this is where you are. Remember, Google Search is integrated with Google Maps and Google My Business. They all work seamlessly in tandem.

So if you can link an address and a zip code to a URL and a place, Google can help people find you specifically. Every time people let Google know their location, it helps people geolocate places of interest, close to wherever they are. So it is very important that you geolocate and connect your URL to your house, as well as to all of the services on the World Wide Web. The most important one is Google My Business (www.google.com/business). This is a free Google utility tool that small businesses benefit from: you share information about your house, its features and what makes you special, you add photos, and you add a pin to Google Maps. Google My Business helps people find you and know more about you. This tool geolocates and puts you on the map and gets you connected.

Now getting on to Google My Business and other sites is important; but consistency is even more important! Remember that in total, the Internet is being searched by a number of computers and the digital world appreciates consistency. So as you're creating your identities on various different sites and loading information in, please make sure it is absolutely consistent. Make sure that names are spelled exactly the same, with the same capitalizations and characters. The street address should be the same. The URL should be the same. Phone numbers and other details should all be accurate, up to date and consistent. When you add pictures, ensure that you tag and input them correctly. A misstep here can confuse the systems and raise a red flag indicating that they're not sure whether you are actually the same organization. Therefore the advantage of being geolocated – of having a specific physical location on the map, becomes paramount.

If the search engines detect discrepancies, they don't think that you're serious. They envision a problem, raise a flag and then create issues. So consistency in creating and updating information on a regular basis, across all the sites that host your information, becomes vitally important. Remember, inconsistency means getting deranked by Google.

Consistency is key, because you should post your information in multiple places to reach your consumer. You should be on all of the free websites, local directories, classified listings sites and search engines. Here is a general list of some of the top web locations where you should have a presence:

- **Google**

  What is the most commonly used search engine? Google. If you are going to be where the people are looking, then you need to prioritize Google. Google even gives you the ability to create your business listing for free with Google My Business (GMB), which will boost your business higher in searches, SEO ranking, reviews, promotions, awareness, and traffic. This service will also allow your business to show up on google maps, and ensures that ideal individuals can easily locate you and get the correct information. Use the Analytics function for a more in depth view of the web traffic to your business. To get more information on this service and register, go here: www.google.com/business/

- **Bing**

  Remember, not everyone uses one kind of search engine. Most Microsoft products such as desktops and tablets have Bing as the default search engine. Much like Google My Business, Bing offers a free service for your business on Bing Places. It boosts your business listing up on their search engine and shows your information on bing maps. For you, it's another great way to advertise and market your business for free. To get more information on this service and register, go here: www.bingplaces.com/

- **Yahoo**

    If you want your company listed on Yahoo along with other directories, Yahoo offers Localworks. This allows you to add business listings, post a listing on yelp, get analytic reports, and any other bells and whistles. However, this is not a free service. Yahoo currently offers multiple pricing plans for you to choose from. To get more information on this service and register, go here: www.smallbusiness.yahoo.com/local

- **Yelp**

    What is the key to getting and maintaining your ideal individuals? Reviews and communication. Yelp is a great resource to utilize for this. With this resource you can easily capture your business reviews which will draw in more of your ideal individuals. Yelp also allows you to communicate back and forth with your consumer so that you can easily answer questions and set up appointments or house tours. To get more information on this service and register, go here: biz.yelp.com/

- **Yellow Pages**

    Your focus should be local. Yellow Pages, being one of the best and most used local search engines, allows you to post a free business listing, respond to your reviews, boost your lead generation, and get marketing resources that will help you in reaching more of your consumers. To get more information on this service and register, go here: www.yellowpages.com

- **Super Pages**

  This local search tool will further assist in boosting your online presence. You can create a business listing, receive reviews, and become a featured business for your area. To get more information on this service and register, go here: www.superpages.com

- **White Pages**

  Get your business information out there and searchable on White Pages. The more local listing and search places you utilize, the better online presence you will have. To get more information on this service and register, go here: www.whitepages.com

- **Merchant Circle**

  Merchant Circle is another great local advertising tool. With this service you can post your business listing, get automated campaign marketing and search engine marketing, post a blog, respond to reviews, and socialize with others in your area and interest. To get more information on this service and register, go here: www. merchantcircle.com

- **LocalStack**

  LocalStack offers a great twist to local search engines by combining and calculating your social media power through your interactions and engagements. Once you social media platform setup and active, this service will help bump your business listing to the top. To get more information on this service and register, go here: www.localstack.com

- **Mapquest**

  Get your business on as many map search services that you can. Mapquest is owned by Verizon, and greatly used by their consumers. Use this service to get your listing out on Mapquest so that you are easy to find for everyone. To get more information on this service and register, go here: www.mapquest.com

- **Insider Pages**

  Under their "Health and Medical" categories, click "see more..." beneath the "Other Health Services" section. If you look closely you will see that there are sections specifically catering to Assisted Living. Having your business listed in these sections will help you find people who are specifically searching for your business. Insider Pages also allows your consumers to review your business. To get more information on this service and register, go here: www.insiderpages.com

- **Ask**

  Ask is another search engine, but it offers no place to put your business information in other than through advertisement. Ask is connected with Google, so your Google rating is reflected with Ask. If you plan on doing advertising, your Google Ads will also be reflected on Ask. To get more information, go here: www.ask.com

- **AOL**

  AOL is another search engine, but it offers no place to put your business information in other than through advertisement. AOL is connected with Bing, so your Bing rating is reflected with AOL. If you plan on doing advertising, your Bing Ads will also be reflected on AOL. To get more information, go here: www.aol.com

- **Blogger**

Your ideal individuals are searching for information. The best way to give them the information relevant to your business is to create a blog that directs back to your website and other social media platforms. Blogger also has analytic reports that shows you where your readers are coming from and their interests. This information will help you to understand how to target your blogs, and ads. To get more information on this service and register, go here: www.blogger.com

- **eLocal**

eLocal is a free business posting and search website with reviews. With this service you also have the option to boost up your posting with their advertising system. To get more information on this service and register, go here: www.elocal.com

- **Foursquare**

Foursquare is a great way for you to promote your business, and it provides you with tons of useful features. With Foursquare you get analytic reports, can reward your consumers, and can even promote your business with area targeted promotion. To get more information on this service and register, go here: www.foursquare.com

- **City Search**

City Search is a local business search service that will help more of your consumers find and get ahold of you. To get more information on this service and register, go here: www.citysearch.com

- **City Grid**

  City Grid is a local business search site which will help you with your business online presence and promotion. It even posts your information on multiple review sites and search engines and directories. To get more information on this service and register, go here: www.citygrid.com

- **Local**

  Local is a local business search site that provides your business information across other sites. To get more information on this service and register, go here: www.local.com

The Internet changes on a regular basis. In the process of writing this book, we found 18 services that let business owners list and customize their businesses for free. However, these are subject to change. Since this is a static published book, this number has changed since we published (even if it's just been a day)! So, I recommend visiting www.millionairemarketerbook.com/RAL to get a master list of all of the websites that you can use along with the hyperlinks so that you can click directly to them, to make your life easier.

You may ask why you need to use all of these other services if Google is the big 500-pound gorilla in the room. In reality, Google only does 64% of the total search. If you work only with Google, (which you should do because they have the best tools), you are still missing in 36% of search results. Therefore it is vital that you go on and create your identity on all of these other services that offer to list and recommend local businesses.

Here is a pro tip: use the same email to log into all of these sites. This adds consistency. Once you've created your identity on Google My Business, one of the things that Google does now is, it takes a look at business reviews and rankings. Having reviews on there once you get yourself set up is vitally important. People who are geographically located in your area can put up reviews about you. Now the search engines can see that you have a geographically located business with people who are geographically co-located in the general area reviewing this business. This gives you higher rankings and your business will come up in suggestions that much more frequently.

Much of the way people are searching online is now about "what's near me?" searches. Google is looking more and more, not only at a geographical radius, but also at how many people rank and review that business. Google has an algorithm for "near me", so a lot of people are now concentrating on getting reviews in the area. This demonstrates that this is a business that's interested in getting local traffic.

As we're talking about local, the URL you're using does not need to be restricted to the name of your RAL home or organization. If you're a virtual company like Facebook, an address such as facebook.com is appropriate. However since you're a local business in a specific geographic area and people may be looking for Residential Assisted Living in, say, Scottsdale, Arizona, your URL does not have to be only the name of your RAL home or company. You can also add Scottsdale or Arizona to the URL. So when people are typing in "Residential Assisted Living in Scottsdale or the Arizona area" into the search box, the URL comes up with that information. It's a pro tip that we use to really help people become searchable.

You could have one comprehensive website that lists all of your RAL homes on different pages, with details and pictures of each. Then you don't need to build a separate website for each. You can register appropriate URLs for each home that includes the city and state, and point them (i.e. redirect them) to the specific pages on your main website.

Here is another pro tip – as you would never give away your house keys or your personal address, you also never never give away your URL. The URL you have, will build your identity; which Google is going to recognize. This is a major asset; one that *you* own. So remember to renew it from time to time. You could register it for a longer duration and even get a discount on the yearly fees. If and when you sell the house, one of the things you're selling along with it, will be the reputation and the ability to drive traffic. So that is a valuable asset that you should always own.

There are people who will get a URL for you and hold it as collateral or own it themselves and try and sell it back to you. This is a bad idea. It is vitally important that you purchase a URL yourself. It is very easy to do. There are a number of online services where you can register domain names. Try GoDaddy.com or Bluehost.com to purchase these URLs yourself because then YOU own it and you can actually get good quality service. Be careful though, many service providers will offer low cost alternatives to get you in. Do not be fooled by low cost alternatives. We'll talk about that in the next chapter.

What is the takeaway? Capitalize on your geographic advantage by setting your house up on Google My Business, as well as other sites, and be consistent throughout.

Invest In Visual Impact

It is said that a picture is worth a thousand words and this is particularly true for the Internet. If you had any doubts about the impact of visual elements, these statistics should put them to rest:

- 84% of communication is expected to be visual by 2018.

- Video content will account for 82% of Internet traffic by 2021.

- 60% of Internet users in the United States choose to watch videos on Facebook in 2017.

- Web pages that have images engage the audience almost 650% more than web pages that only have text.

- Consumers are 85% more likely to make a purchase after watching a product, service, or review video.

- Web pages with video content garner 3 times more backlinks than those only with text content.

- Facebook posts that include images get 87% engagement.

- Tweets with photos get 18% more clicks, 150% more retweets and 89% more likes.

- 60% of buyers are more willing to consider local search results that include images.

- 23% of consumers are more likely to contact a local business whose listing includes an image.

- If your web page has impressive quality photos, you can expect 94% more visitors.

- People recollect 10% of what they hear, and 20% of what they read, but a whopping 80% of what they see.

People are searching for a place for their parents that looks good before they get there: aesthetics, upkeep, ramps etc. for elder access, and surroundings, all matter. It is important to show them what your house looks like, what it's going to feel like.

Images are very important, as the real estate people know. People will look for a geographic address and then start looking at pictures to get a feel of the house. Once they feel like the house is something they could live in, they will then look at the rest of the statistics. However, it is the pictures that convey the all-important first impression, so pictures are worth absolutely every dime you spend on it. I recommend getting a professional person to take pictures of the house: the front and rear of the house, as well as the interiors; particularly of fittings and implements designed for senior living.

The more pictures you can get, the better it is going to be so that people can get a feel before they actually visit and tour the house. They need to get a complete picture of the house. If you can get a video of a walkthrough of the house where you actually walk people from one to another room in the house, this is even better. I've seen some wonderful websites with drone shots as well as such walkthroughs. The important thing here is adequate, high quality visuals to give people a holistic and realistic idea about your house.

It is also important to make sure to keep generic photographs to a minimum. A New York Times article by Nick Bolton suggested that there is a dramatic decrease in interest and activity when people see generic photographs. It is best to use photographs taken of your actual community, your house and the locality. Professional, well lit and well shot pictures increase interest.

You do not want to use pictures of a house that does not equate to where you are because there will be a dissonance between what they've seen on the website and what they physically see when they visit. This can be misleading too. What you want is a seamless experience where they walk into the house and they already feel like they know it because they've seen it online. The familiarity and consistency are reassuring and comforting. Therefore going for good quality video is a step up in a pro tip.

It is also important to make sure that you take images that you have and compress them so that they can work well. We'll talk about that later, but remember this: high quality photographs need to be big enough to be in a high quality format, but small enough to work on the World Wide Web (so that pages load quickly).

What is the takeaway? Invest in good pictures and let them tell your story.

Provide the Experience They Expect

Your online presence should provide the experience that people who are coming there will expect. You do not want people to spend a lot of time waiting for bright pictures or heavy graphics and promotions to load. The user interface should be user friendly, clean and uncomplicated. What they see should be in line with what they will see and hear in person.

What they see should preferably be in line with their cultural references at the time. The last thing you want to do is having kids on skateboards in pictures of your home because it is not the target market; plus it could give the impression that there are potential falling dangers for seniors that lurk around the house! The impression you want to convey is that of caring families taking care of parents. That is a huge difference.

Also, it's important to understand how search results are being rendered. Fewer and fewer people are searching on computers or bigger screens. More and more people are searching on mobiles. In the US roughly 58% of the overall search query is on mobile devices and 40% of all mobile searches have a local intent, i.e. you need to be on Google local search results. 40% of mobile searches have local intent (Google Mobile Moments

Study). This says that not only does your website have to be pretty and clear, it has to be able to be searchable. It also has to be able to talk to people in the way that they're working. Since 58% of the people today are doing research online, it also has to be mobile friendly and mobile interactive.

This means that your website has to look good and function well on computer screens, tablets, phones as well as any type of handheld device. They need to be able to get the information and they need to get it fast. Therefore you have to look at the delivery via your ISP, and also ensure that you have images that can come through both on cellular as well as other devices. Now it is important to also remember that we have to deal with various mobile devices and screen sizes. This becomes more and more important as more and more people search via mobile phones. You need to make your website something called 'responsive', which enables the web layout and spacing to 'respond' to different screen sizes and resolutions.

The advantage of mobile search is that we actually have a geographic location due to phones being GPS enabled. So if you have set up your systems correctly, people will be able to see exactly where you are and the phone will be able to assist in the process of getting them to you. You also have the advantage of being able to geo locate exactly where the customer is and how you can offer your services.

Your user interface must work with all three: desktops, tablets and mobiles. Not getting this right could be quite dire. In one survey, 57% of respondents said that they would not recommend a business with a poorly designed website. And a McKinsey and company study for Google says that 61% of users are unlikely to return to a mobile site they had trouble accessing. 40% users will visit their competitor's website instead. With information available 24/7, you have one opportunity to make a first impression and it is important to make it quick, fast, clean, and exactly what they're looking for. If not, they probably will not return. It takes a lifetime to keep a consumer and a second to lose one. Most possibly, they will also just go to your competitors. They won't bother waiting for you to get it done. There is always someone else.

A web hosting provider with good, fast servers is one of the more important things to be concerned about. Most web hosts provide different levels of service for different rates. The entry-level of service gets you the very basic plan. A simple shared hosting with minimal add-ons. One of our favorites is bluehost, which offers services for $2.99 a month. Now that is an incredibly low number and one should always be skeptical of what one is getting. Read the fine print: What are you paying for? What are you getting for $2.99 or for $7.99 a month? Is it enough? I can tell you, this is not good enough. For an instant on, mobile accessible, media rich environment, you really need to be very careful of what you're doing. You'll probably need to have a hosted system that has a high speed Internet exchange, lots of RAM and Wordpress optimization. In that case, you may be looking at $30 to $40 a month in online fees to make sure it's there.

What is the takeaway? Create a fast, mobile friendly, responsive site that displays your house appropriately and is consistent with your brand, your ideas and your speed so that they don't go to someone else.

Blessed Are The Pessimists,
For They Make Back Ups

In the digital age, life happens like it did earlier. Expect that devices do crash, viruses do get in… you're going to have problems sooner or later. What can you do to prevent the damages of these problems? Have backups of your information.

Have your standby in place, which can get you logged back in to all of your sites. Use an administrative email to log into all of your social sites as well as all of your informational sites. One good email ID that you always have access to, will be your key to it all. Having a complex password that is difficult to guess is the next key.

Rule of thumb: your password should have at least one capital letter, one lowercase letter, a number and a unique symbol as an absolute minimum. It should preferably be more than 10 letters long and not the name of your company, your date of birth, your pet's name, house address or anything simple to guess.

If you're using outside vendors or a third party network, it is important to use a password protection system that allows you to grant access without people actually seeing the password.

There are several such options out there such as UpdraftPlus, BackupBuddy, BackWPUp, BackUpWordPress, Duplicator, VaultPress and many others. There are free as well as paid services. Typically premium or paid services offer better support and functionalities, but in many cases, free services could also work.

You should also have backups of your website content and your social media posts. Websites can become corrupted, computers can crash. So, it is important to back-up your data regularly and consistently. In case something goes wrong, your backup will help restore everything back onto your website. Remember your online presence is one of the most important points of presence you have. Ensure that you backup regularly and consistently at a location different from where your website is. If your website is hacked or if your website goes down, you are able to upload it relatively quickly and get it back online.

You must also have backups of all of your texts and media. There's nothing worse than finding that the images that you've purchased are no longer available while redoing your website. Keeping them in a simple dropbox or other online cloud storage device is a great way of making sure that you always have access to all of your good quality images. For instance, the Google Photo Backup tool will do this automatically for you, so that you never lose any of your precious images. A few minutes of precaution can make a world of difference!

What is the takeaway? Make sure that you have access to all of your content via one trusted, regularly used email ID. Backup your entire system, both websites and images, to make sure you don't lose anything.

Use Other People's Networks
to Promote Yourself

The great promise of social media is that there are vast audiences waiting to be interested, and watch and follow you. This is true to some degree. However, it is also true that lots of people on these networks aren't necessarily interested in following you. A Pew Research Center survey says that 68% of American adults use Facebook. About three quarters of those accessed Facebook regularly, or several times a day. So, there's no question that your demographic is there. 97% of adults between the ages of 16 and 64 say they logged onto at least one social network in the past month (Sprout Social). Nevertheless, social media is not the yellow pages for you. These are not the areas that you should be paying to promote. These are the platforms that you use for social engagement.

People follow people who provide good information. They will not follow people who constantly bombard them with advertising. So you must play the social game correctly to reap its rewards. Many houses just see this as another means of advertising, which is a mistake. They use it as just another means to put information out there, in the assumption that most people want to hear about their good deals. The majority don't. Most people do not want to be sold to on a regular basis. Most people are looking for something of value: want to learn something new, or see something different, informative or entertaining. So, you should absolutely be on Facebook, Instagram, Google Plus and YouTube, but you should be providing value. Now, that's not to say that you shouldn't promote and let people know what's going on, but you have to maintain a balance. If you are promoting more and providing less value, you will have fewer people interested in following you. Do you like to be sold to on a regular basis? Most people don't either.

The other reason that you should really be on the social media networks is this: in 2012, the average Internet user had three social media accounts. Now the average is closer to seven accounts, says Sprout Social, the media management company. There is no one specific social media platform that you should be on. You should aim to be on the social media platform that your target audience uses the most; not necessarily the hottest trending ones The hottest, most trending social media sites are probably the ones that all the kids are on. So if you're on a platform like Twitch to find clients and/or to find your employees, you're probably wasting your time.

Here's a list of the social media networks and what your average target demographic is using:

- Facebook
  - In the US, 68% of adults use Facebook.
  - Worldwide, 76% of Facebook users visit the platform every day.
  - On average, a user spends about 50 minutes each day on Facebook.

- ○ Of the total time spent on mobile devices, 19% is spent on Facebook.

- ○ On average, people access Facebook 8 times a day.

- ○ Over 5 million businesses use Facebook ads to reach their target customers.

- ○ 62% of online marketers say Facebook is the most important social media tool.

- ○ Facebook is the foremost ad channel for both B2C and B2B companies.

- ○ 94% of online marketers are using the Facebook ad platform.

- ○ Facebook ads are projected to generate over $21 billion in the United States alone.

- Google Plus

  - ○ 60% of Internet users on Google Plus are 25-34 years old.

  - ○ Google Plus has 395 million monthly active users.

  - ○ There are about 2 billion worldwide Google Plus users.

  - ○ About half of the total Google Plus users are located in the United States.

  - ○ About 73% of Google Plus users are male.

- Instagram

  - ○ In 6 months during 2016, Instagram users grew by 100 million.

  - ○ There is an overall higher level of social engagement

per post on Instagram than other social media platforms.

- o 18-29 year olds are the primary users of Instagram, 60% of Internet Users
- o Females are 38% more likely to use Instagram than a male.
- o 25% of social media influencers believe instagram is the best for influencer marketing.
- o 38% of Instagram users login to Instagram multiple times a day
- o 51% of Instagram users login to the Instagram app daily.
- o There are 500 million daily users.
- Twitter
  - o 47% of marketers believe Twitter is the best platform for engagement.
  - o 81% of Twitter users check Twitter daily.
  - o 60% of Twitter users tweet once a day.
  - o 15% of Twitter users check Twitter more than 10 times a day.
  - o Twitter increased by 4% in 2017 with 330 million active international users.
  - o There is an average of 208 followers per Twitter user.
  - o 140 million tweets are posted daily.
- YouTube
  - o 1.5 billion monthly active users.

○   30 million daily active users.

○   5 billion videos are viewed daily.

○   Youtube users stay on Youtube for an average of 40 minutes per visit.

○   Every minute, 300 hours of video are uploaded to Youtube.

As you can see, Facebook, Google Plus and YouTube are great places to find the clients that you're looking for. Remember that you should not be targeting the people who will be actually living in your house. You should be targeting the people who are making those decisions. Therefore, finding them on a social media network and having them follow by providing good information on a regular basis allows them to interact with you. So when they're ready to make the decision — and by the way you can actually help them make that decision — they can step right to you for the support instead of wandering around.

Your social media should be seen as a growth strategy; rather like growing a garden. You just don't go out there and start plucking the carrots out of the ground. You need to till the soil, remove the weeds, plant the seeds. You need to keep the birds away from the seeds. You need to water the seeds. You need to care for the seeds and then nurture the saplings. You need to weed regularly to let your plants flourish. Then you've got to make sure they're ready for the actual harvest. That's how you build a good social media network that's interested in you.

What are your potential clients' kids and your potential workers looking for? What information? Give them the opportunity to truly get help from you. Walk them through the process; give them the opportunity to actually come to you. They will be interested and they will check you out.

Your target audience will check out your website(s) and they will also check to see where else you show up. If you only show up as a website for promotion, Google isn't going to like it. YouTube, Facebook, Instagram and Twitter will also not like it because you're not providing value. So when they look you up, you may not rank high simply because you're seen as crass and commercial. So become part of the network, provide specific interest value, and provide local value on a regular basis. This not only increases your social following, it will increase your Internet following and improve your search results.

What is the takeaway? You're expected to provide value on social networks. The search engines expect to see high quality content. Search engines take into account social media following, social media likes, comments, etc. Harness the power of social media to create a community of support and then transform that community into actually customers.

Publish or Perish

This is the rule of the academics and it is now increasingly becoming the rule of people who want Google to play nice with them: all search engines continue to change their algorithms on a regular basis. Following, decoding and predicting these algorithms has become the full time job of SEO experts. Understand that Google does not actually reveal the specifics of their search algorithms. So the only way we can tell is to watch what happens and at least a part of this is just guess work. This is very much of a catch up scenario and it is not ideal. However, there are some established rules because Google recognizes that they cannot look at every one of the 2 billion websites. So they create their algorithms based on how to offer the best, most accurate, relevant and up to date information in response to what people are searching for.

So remember, Google is just trying to provide a good quality service for an individual who is in search of something. So, we in turn have to try and help Google provide them with the right information. If someone is searching for Residential Assisted Living, they're going to be looking for something specific, something helpful and for someone who has knowledge in the area.

As the algorithms in all of the search engines change, there are certain key factors that are important. One of them is to continue to provide good, high quality information to the community. Just putting up a website is not effective. You have to provide content because Google will check your ranking in several areas. It will look to see how often you create and publish content. Is it original? Is it authoritative? Is it accurate and up to date? Are you seen as credible, or knowledgeable about the industry you operate within? Are you providing value or are you just promoting?

It's completely okay to promote on the Internet, but if we want Google to help us get in front of our ideal individuals, then we have to provide value. If you walk into any store and all the salespeople do is tell you what the price is, this is probably going to be inadequate. You may be able to make complete decisions based only on the price of a product if you're going into, say a drug store. However if you're buying a larger, higher quality purchase like a car you need a lot more information about it than just the price. If the salesperson merely tells you what the price is, you're probably not going to stay. If on the other hand the salesperson interacts with you, tries to understand your needs, helps you understand what you want, and then helps you pick the type of vehicle that's right for you, this adds value. You're probably going to: a) spend more time there, b) spend more money there, and c) possibly commit to actually giving a positive review for it.

Google is looking for the same thing with your website. They're looking for someone to understand, to be there, to spend time on the website, to look at multiple pages on the website, to understand and evaluate; and then share that understanding and evaluation by way of a local review. So it is important for you, on a regular basis, to provide value which will determine how well you get ranked overall. Tell people what you do and also provide value to the community where people can read, look at and watch you. This means that people stay on your website longer. Google recognizes this and starts to promote you better.

Search engines are looking for people to tell them how good the website is because they have no ability to do it; at least not yet. No matter how the algorithms change, the need for fresh and original content is an overarching requirement, an unchanging factor. It's important to get on the web as quickly as possible so that you can demonstrate staying power.

You also need to continue to create what Google calls freshness, and freshness is defined as creating new content regularly. This involves updating your pages, providing new information and authoritative material. When updating, focus on useful, core content and not fillers or unimportant boilerplate material. Your core content needs to be about taking care of the greatest generation. Focus on that core content and continue to deliver it.

Keep in mind that if you make small changes on the website, they're probably going to be ignored. The web browsers are comparing old and new. If you need to update a link, consider updating the text around it as well. If you update your phone number, consider refreshing some of the page as well (and remember, if you change your number in one place, change it everywhere else that it exists on the net).

It's also important that there's steady link growth. Computers like steady processes. If you're providing new links, new information consistently, maybe adding and sharing something once every two weeks or so while continuing to link back. This creates organic links back to your website. That's an indication of approval from Google! All other things being equal, links from fresher pages usually get more sales. So in other words, if you've got links coming back to your website from new and exciting pages offering useful information, you're going to get more interest and response.

Engaging metrics are your friends. Find ways to get as many analytic reports about your website that you can. These reports will let provide you a deeper look at how well your site visitors are being engaged and try and figure out what people are interested in. Use that to create new, better, targeted and relevant content.

If you change the topic of a page, some of the older links on the page may lose their value. So in other words, creating more quality material over a period of time gives you greater benefit and older links continue to perform and provide value.

How can you create valuable, good quality content on your website that is regularly updated? One great way to do this is to start a blog. It can be a great way to inform the community, help them learn and make decisions. A blog is a great way to create freshness, update focus, create new backlinks and test engagement material. Not only do you know what to talk about on the Internet, you also know how to speak about each one of your areas. So when potential customers or employees visit, they see you as knowledgeable, authoritative and sympathetic. They see that they can work well with you!

What is the takeaway? Provide value to get better results. The more you provide value, the more the search engines will appreciate your time.

Integrate Online and Offline

Having a good offline presence or having a good online presence is great. However, integrating and using both to create a positive and powerful marketing experience is something that has a multiplicative effect. In other words, if they find you online and come to your house, does your house look like the pictures? Do they recognize the people, the staff shown on the website? We like to go to a place and then meet people that we actually recognize. So do you have photographs of several of the people that they're going to meet? Are you, as the owner, going to be there? If so, your photographs help because they get the opportunity to recognize you and feel more comfortable!

If they have seen you in several other areas, it may feel like they already know you. This familiarity is valuable because it is reassuring. We set up video processes where people actually feel like they know the individual. The videos provide specific content, while allowing a personal connection and understanding to form. Several of our VIP customers have been stopped in their local towns where people feel like they know them because they've watched all of their content.

It used to be that people would get excited because they

were Facebook friends with this individual. Even though this individual may have hundreds or thousands or millions of Facebook followers, that individual connection still matters. A YouTube survey dating back to the late 2000s said that most people couldn't tell the difference in authority of someone on the computer and someone on TV. You will be seen as having that authority; it will be transferred over to your sales position if you do it correctly.

It is also recommended that your physical brochure should look like your website. It should have the same information. It should have the same look and feel. It should have the same logo, and same color scheme. So that what they see online and what they see offline is in a continuum. What they see in the house and what they see online also has to be consistent; in continuum. So pulling it all offline, you want to be able to have a high touch ability as well. Have a simple brochure that they can take away with them. It doesn't have to be complex. A three fold brochure is perfectly good; a little reminder that they can take away. Also having a visiting card with the same color scheme and logo that's on the website and on all the print materials, makes you come across as a professional, trustworthy organization.

Remember you want clear, bright images that are easy to see, and content that's easy to read. You want a clear, large font size that is easy to read, keeping in mind that there will be a lot of older people visiting your site. You don't want to put them off with small, busy, difficult to read content. Having a high quality full color brochure or at least a trifold is very useful.

Here is a pro tip you can use - one page of the brochure can be kept blank white, so that visitors can take notes or add any additional information they need. This way they get to take home a brochure with your information on one side and their personal notes on the other side.

In my experience, this integrative approach between online and offline identities is very beneficial and conveys a very positive message. The printed material such as brochures, visiting cards and letterheads etc. don't have to be expensive. Please go to www.millionairemarketerbook.com/RAL to find a list of our favorite vendors where you will find some affordable options.

Here's an interesting idea: sometimes it's the subliminal materials that can really be effective. So if you pick up a card, how does that card feel? Many of your clients will want a physical card because that is just how they operate. When they pick it up, does it feel like it's an inexpensive card or does it have some weight to it? Is it a slightly heavier bond paper? Does the paper feel like it is good quality? The cost differential between inexpensive and high quality card paper is not much, but it can have a powerful psychological effect on the people.

We have a tendency to print on whatever kind of light-weight paper is available, even the print copy paper, but if you spend a few more dollars, this conveys a very different impression. A few more dollars per ream of paper, you can get higher quality paper, with brighter whites. We suggest 96 or above in white brightness. It's just a slightly more intense white. It's not as gray. If you put this white paper up against most copy paper, the copy paper looks gray by contrast. That heavier weight paper again feels like it is quality without much cost differential.

I personally love to have very thick, very heavy cards, firstly because of how they stand apart from all of the light, cheap cards, and secondly because they last longer. If you hand over a high quality card, people will look at it. I've actually had people comment on the weight of a card I've handed over. It kind of makes them liken it to the 'weight' of the business. We have a list of vendors on the website www.millionairemarketerbook. com/RAL attached to this, which we update on a regular basis to make sure that you get high quality, durable products.

Another offline/online process and great technique is to take several of your articles out to local news areas. Take an article and see if you can get it into your local websites. If there's a chamber of commerce, a local, state or county authority website, maybe you can have your presence noted there. These people are dying for new content and if you can provide content about your target market, people will be searching for it. The advantage for them is you're giving it away for free; the advantage for you is, you earn credibility and get visibility. At the bottom you have your name, who you're with and a URL pointed back to your website. Your target audience gets access to something that is useful and relevant to them. Win-win all around!

This integration now produces three vital effects:

- Firstly, you're spreading your message to other people and you're doing it for free. You're providing high quality value on a regular basis and you are getting people to link back to the main page on your website in case they want more information.

- Secondly, the search engines recognize this as quality content pointing to a particular website; so they presume that your website is high quality as well. It is a good idea to get all of the information in the area pointed to you on a regular basis. So take the content stuff that you publish, rewrite it slightly and then have it re-published.

- Thirdly, the more you get your business out there, the more opportunity you have to connect with other experts in the industry. This may lead to offline marketing opportunities such as talking at conferences.

What is the takeaway? Let your online and offline efforts display uniformity and be in sync. Pick higher quality stationery, and republish rewritten articles in local websites or publications.

Advanced Technique: The Value Funnel

Websites are a great area to gain information and to start a conversation, but without the control of the conversation, this is of limited value. So we go out and try to increase website traffic, i.e. get more visitors to the website. The challenge here is that those people are controlled by an external force. If you're advertising on Facebook or on YouTube, those people are members of YouTube, Facebook or whatever the social media network. If they're coming in through Google, then Google knows who they are; you don't, and it doesn't allow you to create a conversation.

So, we use an advanced technique — creating a value funnel — which provides an opportunity for people dropping by your website to gain more information. Once your contact information is up and available, your goal should be to capture the consumers information and get them to call or drop by for a visit. Certainly a human touch for this sort of sale is vastly important. However, sometimes they're not ready.

Sometimes they're in the research stage. At this research stage, we may not be able to get them to call immediately, but we want to demonstrate to them that we're interested, that we can give them value and that they will be taken care of. So, we try to give them a second option. Option number one is always to get them to contact you and try and make the sale, but if they're not quite ready to pull the trigger and talk to someone, we don't want to lose them.

This is where the value funnel comes into play. The value funnel is basically offering them a second opportunity to get some more information, something that you think they would need. For example, it could be as simple as a free to download PDF (Portable Document Format) document, seven to 12 pages long, well written, well formatted, and with some high quality color graphics (because colors on the Internet is free). These, by the way, can be stock images because the expectation is merely that of good quality material, not necessarily what the person will be paying for. If you can use actual images of your house, facilities and your people, that would be great; but it isn't absolutely necessary. Stock images are as acceptable here.

The pdf topic could be something like (and this could be my favorite): *The 7 Things You Should Look For in Residential Assisted Living Before You Buy*. Make a list of those 7 things and explain why they're important. Explain how to go about achieving each of those aims. Other good ones are: *6 Indicators That It's Time To Get Mom and Dad Into Residential Assisted Living*, or *5 Tips To Keeping Sane During The Transition to Residential Assisted Living*. These are great topics. They are targeted exactly to the people looking to start this process and answer actual questions they have in their mind.

This pdf also gets you their email address. Near the download PDF link, would be a little area that asks for the name and email address of the site visitor, to have the document delivered. The system then automatically sends an email to your site visitor that says, "Here is the material you requested, and by the way, we're going to send you some other things" or something to that effect. So if they are doing *The 7 Things You Should Look For in Residential Assisted Living Before You Buy*, you should follow that up a couple of days later with some more emails, each one talking about the transition stages: what they need to do, or how they may be feeling when they're doing this for their parents. So you're providing this information, offering reassurance, providing guidance, and delivering good quality content via email!

Now email systems are calibrated in a way that they will send more of what people are interested in. If your site visitors are expecting your email again, when your email does pop up, they will click on it, and they will continue to receive more of what they see as valuable to them. With each email, you're providing them some more information and adding value. You're delivering good information and they are now becoming familiar with you. They start to care. So, even if they haven't made the decision yet, when they do decide, you're at the top of their mind. This is an easily automated system that doesn't require much effort, but can create huge benefits in the long term; creating a much more effective way of starting and maintaining an ongoing conversation on a regular and consistent basis.

Advanced Technique: YouTube Advertising & Geo Location

YouTube is the second largest search engine in the world. It processes 3 billion searches every month, has 1 billion unique monthly visitors (which is one of every 2 Internet users) and has about 6 billion hours of videos viewed every month. So clearly, many people will be searching that area! Creating a geographically targeted search can help. If people are on YouTube and searching for your information, you can actually provide them an advertisement with geolocation.

So imagine creating a video of your house, talking about the benefits, talking about why the house is good, where it is, and what's available, very similar to what you do on the website, but in video format. This could be you speaking directly to the camera or you can use slides with a voiceover. It doesn't really matter. One of the most important things is that the video has good audio. The audio is almost *more* important than the video.

So you can create this video, and then go onto Google Adwords and actually offer this video to people of the specific demographic within your geographic area. So in other words, anyone who is searching for general information about "assisted living" or other keywords that you define, and are within a hundred miles of your geographic location, this video will be targeted at them. They are looking for assisted living for seniors and your video is right there for them to view. It is appropriately targeted for their requirements too!

The next aspect to keep in mind is appropriate labeling. You have to label and geotag it in a way that if people are searching for it, it comes up in the Google search as well. So if the searcher has shown interest in a certain video, Google will come up with more videos like that. On Google, if people search for your town and Residential Assisted Living or whatever it's called in your state, your video is likely to pop up. Creating the video and delivering it to multiple areas at the same time gives you the opportunity to get in front of more people who are looking for that information.

Some people like to listen to audio. Some people like to watch a video. Some people like to read the written word. A YouTube video has something for all three if you put printed text on the actual screen. Increasingly now, people go to YouTube to find out how to do things. So creating one of those how-to videos for your Residential Assisted Living facility could be a great idea. Maybe something on the lines of *How To Prepare Your Parents For A Move To Assisted Living.*

Advanced Technique: Article Creation for Backlinks

As we discussed in the Integrate Online and Offline chapter, creating articles is one very valuable way of providing content, but you don't have to just put that content on your website. There are hundreds of websites looking for valuable content from experts. So, if you can provide high quality articles on a regular and consistent basis to these sites, the local paper, or to local information sites, all of these point back to your website. It does three things:

- Firstly it creates the impression of you being the local expert and people will want to come to you.

- Secondly, it gives you the advantage of new people finding you, not necessarily on your website, but at other locations or sites that they trust.

- Thirdly, the incoming links from external sources leading to your website give you advantages on Google search rankings.

These are all valuable, and it's just as easy to take this idea offline as it is to use it online.

Your online content can also be put to work offline. Explore local areas, volunteer organizations that have weekly meetings, and so on. These weekly meetings have the advantage of always needing content and can include the YMCA, the Rotary Club, the Knights of Columbus, the Elks Club, and many other fraternal clubs, as well as coffee houses, libraries, etc. For a list of contact information that we've continued to keep updated go to our website at www.millionairemarketerbook.com/RAL.

It's very simple to have a 10 to 15 minute presentation setup. It doesn't have to be about your house, but can be about anything that is useful or informative: resources for seniors, devices and home alterations to manage reduced mobility, nutrition tips etc. The advantage of that is three-fold:

- Firstly, you again get in front of local people who may have an elderly parent(s) or may know someone with elderly parent(s). People in volunteer organizations usually have higher incomes, more interest in the community and greater social networks. If someone else is having a problem, they may recommend you.

- Secondly, they will advertise club events and link back to you in their various websites and on social media. Again, an organization linking back to you saying you're about to come and you're about to speak, linking back to your house and your quality content, increases your links and your ability to get more links. It also demonstrates the interest that organizations have in you.

- Thirdly, your presentation is also an opportunity to take along and distribute your brochure. Your brochure speaks about your facility and also has a follow-along document, which allows people to write, interact directly, and add notes.

You do not necessarily have to do a heavy or very long pitch. All you have to do is, master a short 10 to 15 minute presentation in front of a number of people and answer some quick questions or find someone who can do this. Your audience will be encouraged to go back to your website to get more information and you can build up a conversation with them. This is a key technique of Guerrilla marketing that many people miss out on.

Advanced Technique: Stacking

Once you've got your website in place and you start using these techniques on a regular basis, pick one to begin with, and then start stacking it. The information that you're putting out on a regular basis on your website as well as on social media can also be delivered to other platforms where you can become visible. The beauty of this process is that you may only have to make the effort once and then leverage this process for all the other platforms.

Now that you have the email address of visitors on your site (remember we spoke about the value funnel?) you can give them even more content. The more they feel like you're supporting them, as opposed to selling to them, the more they'll be interested in engaging with you and working with you.

As these techniques stack, they continue to become more powerful marketing tools. Soon you will find that you're outstripping other people's marketing and you're doing less work at it. Because now, you're starting to leverage the power of your website, the power of the Internet, the power of the search engines, the power of social media, the power of local media, and the power of the interested parties, all of which will come together for you and continue to gain momentum.

The key here is consistency. If you start this process, follow through and make it a consistent practice. Don't overwhelm yourself; do what you can. You'll find that everyone rewards consistency. So, the more consistent and regular you are, the more the system and people see and reward your consistency.

Imagine a scenario where someone visits a website that was only put up a week earlier. They may have trouble trusting that, but if they check out a blog and see that it has been providing good quality information to the community for years, that the local chamber of Commerce has had you speak and the local Rotary Club has had you speak; you're mentioned in the state newspaper and the county magazine or the local online magazine. All of a sudden, your credibility on the Internet goes up. Likewise, it also goes up in the eyes of everyone else!

This is a process that takes time, but if you're consistent with it and do one or two things a month only, you become much more of the 'leading expert', and all of a sudden everyone is flocking to you! Not necessarily because you're any better, but because you're *seen* as the expert in the industry and everyone wants to work with the best in the business.

Advanced Technique:
Facebook Value Sequence

It is important to talk about paids advertisement, because paid advertisements *work*. One of the best techniques to get people integrated into your process once you have some of the other advanced techniques in place, is to opt for Facebook advertising. Here you can target people who are interested in your subject and in your local area. It's relatively inexpensive to get people's views. It is difficult to get them to follow. So this technique relies on you already having a large amount of good quality content.

Once you have that good quality content you also have the ability to geolocate people in a specific income stream, within a specific age group, living in a specific geographic area with possibly specific interests, and target them to provide them more information. This information is all about getting them to recognize you as an expert. This is a long term play, not a short term plan. It is the ability for you as an individual to interact with them, give them material that they may be thinking about.

You're offering specific solutions for aging parents, people who now need some help. You're offering answers to children looking to learn how to discuss difficult subjects with an aging parent, those wondering how to move their parents from the home that they've lived in all their life in to a new and vibrant community. You're informing them about *"The 7 Things You Should Look For in Residential Assisted Living Before You Buy"* via your blog as we discussed before. Each one of these would be an article or articles that you create.

Instead of selling directly, you simply provide information. You put an ad on Facebook which, when they click on, takes them over to an actual article on your website. If you're using the value funnel technique, they may provide their email to get more information! So you can strategically bring people in, provide them an opportunity to read and learn something, and then provide them an opportunity to go deeper by giving them the email option.

Now the advantage is that you can target exactly who you want and where, so you're not advertising to all the Facebook users around. You're focused on giving Facebook ads to specific people and delivering them that quality content. They see your ad, want more information and then they come to recognize you. You can do this really cheaply - each person clicking on your ad is a few cents apiece! Then you'll have a mailing list that you can continue to have conversations with. That stacking will support you in the long run and also provide value in the short run.

This is an advanced technique. You need to be solid in your process and have lots of vital information. These people will be computer and Internet savvy users and will probably check to see if you're on Facebook and other social media networks; so if you are and you're providing good content, more and more people will come to you.

You see how this system can reap rich dividends o period of time? This is a wonderful and inexpensive way or indirect advertising to drive more people to your website, while offering quality content and getting quality exposure. We can certainly do Facebook advertising directly to people who may want it, but it's becoming more and more difficult. It's hard to target exactly who needs this material. It's easier if you offer them something that is a little tangential in the path to making a decision. This can be useful information that helps them make that decision.

Help them make the right decision as opposed to advertising directly to them. You may spend a lot of money doing that without seeing commensurate results, but remember, this is a long term plan of gaining unshakably positive reputation. In the long run, the efforts and the money spent will be well worth it.

If you're still wondering if you should create a Facebook business page or if Facebook advertising is for you, think about those startling Facebook statistics we discussed earlier. View them again, but this time consider and reflect on how these statistics can apply to your online, marketing, and advertising presence:

- In the US, 68% of adults use Facebook.

- Worldwide, 76% of Facebook users visit the platform every day.

- On average, a user spends about 50 minutes each day on Facebook.

- Of the total time spent on mobile devices, 19% is spent on Facebook.

- On average, people access Facebook 8 times a day.

- Over 5 million businesses use Facebook ads to reach their target customers.

- 62% of online marketers say Facebook is the most important social media channel.

- Facebook is the foremost ad channel for both B2C and B2B companies.

- 94% of online marketers are using the Facebook ad platform.

- Facebook ads are projected to generate over $21 billion in the United States alone.

Advanced Technique: Using your URL to drive traffic

One of the fastest ways to drive traffic is to create multiple URLs. If you're in a specific town and you know there's interest in Residential Assisted Living, then creating Residential Assisted Living Scottsdale, or Residential Assisted Living Tuscaloosa or Residential Assisted Living _____ (insert city name here) as one of your URLs will increase your search capability. When someone is searching for an assisted living home for their parents, they will likely search for their location and "assisted living" or "residential assisted living". I recommend not only using the name of your company as URL but also using the other search criteria. Having a URL with the keywords that your ideal individuals will be searching will put your business at the front of the list.

This has to be done fast. You have to capture it and it has to have the URL information. You can, of course, redirect these URLs to the specific pages of your main website. You need not create complete websites for these generic sounding URLs. These are to help gain traction in search rankings and could eventually also show up on the first page of search results. Creating this gives you an additional search capability; another advanced technique you can use.

Advanced Technique: Using Google Adwords / PPC

The most expensive and difficult advertising to do, is actually buying PPC (Pay Per Click) ads. These are the ads that pop up when you search in Google. So if you were to search for Residential Assisted Living Texas, you will see people who are buying ads directly for that. This is an expensive way of doing it because every time someone clicks on it, you have to pay, and if it is not geolocated very well to your area, you're going to be paying for a lot of site visitors who are not interested in your place. The key is to get your ad campaign designed right.

PPC ranks you better. It puts you at the top of the ranking but it is an expensive process and therefore testing is required. It may take you several months to figure out how to do the best PPC ads and how to integrate them. It takes time and you have to be very specific about exactly how you're doing it, so that Google likes you. It starts with creating a Google Adwords account and entering all your site information.

There are a lot of tools integrated within Google Adwords that help you shortlist the keywords you need to target. You can find search frequency data for your keywords and target audience in the geolocation you're targeting with ease on the system. You can start with a few test ads with low per click rates, see the results vis-a-vis the expenses, and make adjustments as you go forward. This is something that you get better at with practice.

Make sure that your legal disclosures and disclaimers are all set up on the website to avoid any hassles. If you're unsure about getting started with Google Adwords, you could seek professional help for this to begin with or do your research online. In case, if you still have doubts about the effectiveness of Google Adwords, these statistics will help open you up to the idea:

- Consumers are 155% more likely to search for brand-specific and segment-specific terms in Google, compared to other terms.

- 89% of the traffic generated by Google ads is not likely to be replaced by organic traffic if ads are paused.

- It has been seen that when it comes to search terms that indicate high commercial intent, the top three ad spots get 40% of the clicks.

- 98% of searchers choose a business from page 1 of Google search results.

- On average, businesses make double the amount they spend on Google Adwords.

- 70% of mobile searchers will call a business directly from Google Search results.

- 70% of mobile searches result in action being taken within 60 minutes.

- 650,000 apps serve Google ads.

- Google ads reach 90% of Internet users.

BONUS: The Blink Test

Now here's a bonus section that'll help you establish your RAL (Residential Assisted Living) home in the minds of your target consumers. This doesn't just apply to one of your homes, you can use these bonus tips to create a formidable umbrella brand for all the homes you own. This section will show you exactly what it takes to gain credibility, memorability and reliability in the eyes of your ideal individuals, and it's all based on some key principles of branding. Many of our homeowners hold off on putting out their dream RAL business because of a branding element. We're going to put an end to that right now and we are going to simplify the whole game.

So, what is the game? You can build your brand just like the hometown it's a part of using the 10 landmarks of branding. For this bonus, we will touch upon the first three branding landmarks of Name, Tagline, and Logo in the following chapters.

- **Name.** Does the name really matter? A name can build you up or tear you down. How does your brand name affect your target customers?

- **Tagline.** It is important to have a tagline that sparks emotion, fulfills the target customer's wish, is memorable, and is new but familiar.

- **Logo.** Your logo is the flag of your community. Use that design to unite your consumers, get them to embrace your brand and your home. Let it embody the values and ethics that your RAL homes stand for, so that when people see your logo, they see a community for their parents; the one they've been looking for.

The Blink Test: The Secret Power Of Naming

In this chapter, we'll talk about how you can use the secret power of naming to create the right kind of allure for your target customers and jet fuel your Residential Assisted Living home and brand.

People often ask: Does the Name really matter?

There is an enormous amount of evidence of companies that had a product that tanked due to poor naming. Torro had a snowblower that they wanted to be geared towards single women, and they called it Snow Pup. And guess what, it tanked! They later changed the name to Snow Master. These women were already feeling like pups, like they couldn't master the snow in their driveway. All it took was a change in name to change the impression, the perspective, and the sales went up. That's just one of thousands of cases like that.

You want the answer to the question "What's in a name?" It is a call into being of a greater future. So when you're naming your RAL home or business, think about what greater future you want to call into being, not only for yourself and your company, but for everyone who will be living in your home, everyone who will be a part of the community you're creating. You want your target individuals to follow your brand, enter your home, and hopefully take up permanent residency as brand loyalists.

How Do You Get the Name That Stands Out From the Hundreds of Ads We See a Day?

Naming has never been more important. It just gets more and more crucial to the life of your brand. It's not like the old times where we'd all be in a movie theater for two hours committed to the journey. Now we're on the Internet, we're surfing, we don't care. We don't think twice before flitting from one website to another.

One brand to another. We are seeing 5000 ads a day. We are professional deleters. You've got to make people care with your brand name. You've got to instill an emotion in their heart and compel them to join your brand, and you only have a few seconds. That's your Blink Test.

Take YouTube for example, they have ads before their videos that are about 15 to 20 seconds long, but they allow you to skip out after three to five seconds. Why do they do this? Because they don't want you to skip out of YouTube altogether. They know they've only got three to five seconds to keep you. YOU only have three to five seconds to keep your target individuals.

Compel Them With Your Name.

Let's talk about how you can make your brand name compelling, what you can do to not lose them at the name itself, and how not to toss away this opportunity by simply describing the home and the features or the one key benefit. Use the name to compel them into a greater future. You can do that by using the five attractions of every great name. We will go into that in just a minute.

First let's talk about the three brand killing mistakes that most entrepreneurs make and how you can avoid them. Here they are:

1. **Not thinking big enough.** You see, great names work for you 24/7 and bad names work against you 24/7. So don't think only of your current city and locality and what works there. Think big. Tomorrow you could have homes across many cities and states, maybe even other countries.

   So pick a name that's not offensive to an entire culture. Did you know that IKEA has a work bench called "Fartfull." Would you like to buy a bench by that name? There are some other ones too. "Sake" means urine in Russian. "Waterpik" means morning erection in Danish. Everybody knows about 'Nova Chevy'. Nova is no go.

   So, make sure that you use resources like freedict. com to check the meaning of your Name in other languages. Don't be gross. Don't offend an entire community of people. Think big. Think global.

2. **Being too insider.** Having a name that only a few would understand the relevance of isn't the right way to go. You want to appeal to a big audience. Think big.

When you are coming up with your name, don't use a little insider, trendy sort of buzzword in your industry. Another reason is that trend is going to be so yesterday so very soon. I would compel you to think bigger than the way everyone's thinking right now at this moment.

3. **Being too vague.** I think people are being compelled by SEO to name their company or product a search engine optimization type of name. Imagine a company called "Dog Training Academy". It is like naming a sneaker "Rubber Soled Shoe". You know it's not compelling. It's not going to get people to join your community. Don't go for vague and generic names. They are not compelling at all. They don't engage the target customers.

5 Attractions of a Great Name

You want a name that is engaging. So let's talk about how to do that. How do you call into being a greater future with your name? You use the five attractions of every great name, which are:

1. **Emotion.** You want your name to instill an emotion in the heart of everyone that sees it and you want it to be the emotion that they're most craving. What emotion do you think your target audience, the people looking for Assisted Living facilities for their parents, is looking for? Security? Compassion? Care? Love? You want a name that instills one of these emotions because when we purchase anything we only do so emotionally.

It's been proven in MRI scans, actually, that when

you're making any decision, it is the emotional center of the brain that's doing it for you. In fact, they put people under brain scans and had them look at brands and the same exact areas lit up as when they looked at pictures of their best friends and loved ones. This is the kind of bond that you can have with your target individuals when you use the attraction of emotion. This is the most important feature your name needs to have. Emotion. That's the name game. Get emotional.

2. **Wish Fulfilled.** Every movie, every play, every book you've ever read, or seen, or shared with anyone there is a wish fulfilled and you get to fulfill a wish vicariously by watching the characters go through the paces. So too with your name. It should be a wish fulfilled.

For example, Payless is a wish fulfilled. Imagine a mom with 2 kids on a tight budget. The kids need new shoes, but she knows they'll outgrow them in a couple of months. So she wins by going to Payless. She becomes the hero of her story. That's her wish fulfilled to pay less.

Understand, what are the struggles your target customers are facing? What is the wish they are looking to fulfill? Let your name reflect that.

3. **Memorable.** There are some tricks about being memorable. You want it to be easy to say, and easy to pronounce. You don't want your old customers struggling to tell others where they are going to be living, right? Keep this in mind when choosing your name. Don't choose something exotic or complicated or long that they cannot remember or repeat.

4. **Easy to Spell.** People, especially older folks, shouldn't have to guess its spelling. Imagine you have a name that you wanted and find that it's taken, because almost every .com is taken. Then imagine you try to name it that same name but you change the spelling. Every time you tell someone "oh I'm at homekare .com but I spell it with a k." They have to remember an extra thing and out it goes. They're not going to remember it. Whereas, it would be much better if you said "I'm at homecare .com because we care for you like you would expect at home." That would be a much more memorable way to introduce your .com name.

5. **New but Familiar.** You want a balance of new but familiar. In every story someone new comes to the familiar town or someone leaves their familiar town to go somewhere new. New but familiar. That's an adventure.

So, you want your brand name to be an adventure that people are excited about because it's new, but one they're not too afraid to embark upon. They can anchor themselves in some kind of familiarity. That won't be familiar enough for the general population.

You want to have a healthy balance of new but familiar. If it's too new people, especially older folk, are going to be afraid to go. They'll think think they don't belong there. If it's too familiar, they probably won't feel excited enough. It won't sound special and appealing. So you need to hit a healthy balance being new but familiar with your choice of name.

Ask yourself these questions:

When you're going over your list of names that you've been pouring over and you are trying to decide what to call your RAL home brand, ask yourself how it would score on all of these five attractions:

- Is it emotional?
- Is it a wish fulfilled?
- Is it memorable?
- Is it easy to spell?
- Is it a healthy balance between new but familiar?

When you hit the bull's eye on the five attractions of a great name, you've found your name.

Is your name available?

People wonder if they should only get a .com, even if the name they want is taken. What about a .net or .org or .biz or …? No, .com is still very much seen as the thing to have. It's like real estate. You want to be in the good neighborhood and .com's the good neighborhood. You want to sound like a legit business, and so .com is the way to go. If your favorite name is taken, move on and go back to the five attractions of every great name and create new lists of names that you love.

Lastly, another tip about naming is to check if your name is available on all the social media platforms. You can use www.nameck.com and quickly check for this vital aspect.

What is the takeaway?: The Dos And Don'ts Of Naming

- Don't be vague.
  - Do have a clear brand promise.
- Don't just describe the stuff.
  - Do be emotional. We all make emotional decisions so be emotional in your naming.
- Don't be like everyone else using the buzzwords that everyone else is using.
  - Do be highly memorable: easy to say, easy to spell, easy pronounce, and easy to share.
- Don't insult an entire country.
  - Do check the meaning of your names in other languages and other cultures.

I am dedicated to helping you name your dream RAL business. You see, I don't think it's a coincidence that you're getting this message right now. I think you were made to get the secret power of naming. I don't work with just anyone. I am looking for the dreamers, the creators, the inventors, the caretakers of humanity, because when you work with me you become a part of my family and my family is made up of smart, compassionate men and women.

You are ready to run an RAL home that people will long to live in, that people will recommend to others, where there's joy and love and care and quality.

The Blink Test: The Secret Power Of Taglines

In this chapter, you will learn how to use the secret power of taglines to jet fuel your RAL brand, how to get free advertising for life, and how to create a tagline that doesn't suck the energy right out of your brand. Let's get started.

How do you get free advertising for life?

Just like in the name chapter, here you use the four attractions of every great tagline; emotion, a wish fulfilled, memorable, and new but familiar.

- **Emotion.** What emotion is your RAL home promising its residents? Make sure your tagline echos that emotion, and doesn't contradict what you've achieved by finding a great name.

  Your tagline needs to further reinforce the emotion that your name evokes. Is it one of security? Of compassion and care? Of company? Of joyous days? Zero in on the emotion your name evokes, and create a tagline that further preserves it into the minds of your target individuals.

- **Wish Fulfilled.** What wish is your target audience looking to fulfill? You've found it when deciding your name, and you need to further the promise of that wish being fulfilled by your RAL home with the tagline you choose.

- **Memorable.** How to ensure that your tagline is memorable? Keep it short and catchy. Make it emotional. Make it resonate with your target individuals.

- **New but Familiar.** Strike a nice balance between new and familiar, not just with your name, but also your tagline. Make sure it's exciting enough to pull them in, yet not overwhelming enough to keep them out.

If your tagline can hit all four of these attractions; emotion, a wish fulfilled, memorable, new but familiar, then you've got a bullseye.

How to Create a Tagline That Doesn't Suck the Energy Out of Your Name

How do you get a tagline that doesn't suck the energy right out of your name? You use the four S's of not sucking.

- **Story.** The story is the most important aspect. Your tagline needs to tell a story. One of adversity or struggles, and then a victory over them. That's the classic story of a hero. And who doesn't want to be the hero of their own lives and worlds?

  Can you see your target customer doing the victory dance through your tagline? Does it inspire a hero's story. One of overcoming hurdles and emerging strong? That's what it should!

- **Short.** Taglines are short when every word counts, not by the word count, necessarily. You want every word to have an impact on the target customer. It needs to be short and impactful. It needs to snap you awake. However, a longer tagline can still work if every word counts, if it's memorable, and if it tells a story high on emotion.

- **Simple.** Keep it simple. Your tagline is not there to explain everything that you do. It's not there to describe the service. What it is, is an invitation into your home. It's to set the tone for the way of life inside of your home. It's not saying everything that your home is about. It's almost impossible to do. What you want to do is send out an invitation through your simple but emotional tagline for people to join your community.

- **Savory.** Be savory in your tagline. Engage the senses. Make people see, feel, hear, touch, imagine their life in your community, in your RAL home. Does your tagline do that? They need to feel right now what living in your home might feel like for them. They should want to know more. They should want to come right over.

Double check your tagline to make sure you have met all the four S's of not sucking the energy right out of your name. Let me also say this: these four S's of not sucking the life out of your brand are not hard and fast rules but more of a guideline. Ultimately, you need to find what works best for you.

Invite people to the way of life inside your RAL home. If your tagline is a little bit long, but it's extremely savory and it hits the story like a bull's eye, then you've got yourself a great tagline. Remember that great taglines work for you 24/7 and bad taglines work against you 24/7.

What is the takeaway?: The Dos And Don'ts Of Taglines

People want to call your brand home. They want to feel that they have arrived in a place that they know, love and trust. Let's go over the dos and don'ts of creating your branding landmark of your tagline.

- Don't be like everyone else.
  - o Do be highly memorable, through using emotion, being unique, and being savory.
- Don't describe everything that you do.
  - o Do invite us to the home. Let us know what kind of community you have to offer.
- Don't count every word.
  - o Do make every word count.

The Blink Test: The Secret Power Of Logos

In this chapter, you will get the secret power of your logo, the four S's of not sucking the life right out of your brand name, and the three types of logos that you can use.

Many people question, "Do logos really matter? Do I have to really think into this in detail?" Well I ask you, how many people have lived and died to defend a flag? Your logo is the flag of your community. Use that design to unite them, to embody your values and ethics, so that when they see your logo, they see a community, the one they've been looking for. They see a solution to the things that are missing in their life, and they want to join that community. That is the secret power of logos.

Very often, people wear your logo on their person. Your staff, your caretakers, even your residents could be wearing clothes with your logo on them. That's free advertising. Walking around advertising to every single person around their allegiance to your RAL home, to your community. Their identity is now with you.

That's exceedingly powerful. That's exactly what you want. You want a following. We're 50 times more likely to buy when we hear about something from our friends, when we see it around us.

It this human emotion that you want to tap into and take very seriously.

The Secret Power of Logos.

Your logo should be consistent. They're repetitive. We are visual creatures and all our decisions are made emotionally. We can be logical later and give you a logical reason why we decided something, but really, we did it because we were touched emotionally in some way.

So with your logo, make sure that you are telling the same story that you began with the name. One that has the same emotional impact. If you can name the emotion for the name, and you can name it for the tagline, and you can name it for the logo, you're in great shape.

The 5 S's to Create Logos That Don't Suck the Life Out of Your Name

Let's get right into the five S's of not sucking the life right out of your brand name.

- **Simple**. Clarity out performs cleverness every time. So, keep it simple. That should be your main objective.

- **Second look.** Make them lean in with your logo. Make them say "Hmm, that looks interesting, that looks like me."

- **Soloist.** Don't be a copycat. Research all of your competitors and don't do what they're doing. Do something that's unique to call your target individuals away from them and into your RAL home.

- **Symmetry.** Employ the magic and mastery of symmetry, which is in every living thing.

- **Story.** Make sure that your logo continues your brand story that you started with. The name, followed by the tagline, and now the logo.

Keeping it Simple.

Remember clarity out performs cleverness every time. So how can you keep it simple? You could keep in one color. Which color best represents the energy and the feeling inside of your RAL home? We all have a common language when it comes to color.

Another way you can be simple is reduce the energy or emotion or promise of your brand to its most simplest format. Like Nike or Amazon. So, keep it simple. You don't want to have too many details. You don't want to have too many colors. You could use one or two. You could even have a black and white logo to keep it very simple. If you look at some of the biggest brand names, they only use one to two colors. So, make sure that you keep it simple.

Garnering a Second Look.

Perhaps your logo means one thing but when you look at it a little bit longer, you could find another meaning in it. People look twice and think, "Oh that's cool. Now I know. I really am feeling you." This might seem counterintuitive to what I just said about keeping it simple, but I want to teach you all the tricks so that you can create magic with your logo. Sometimes you need to break a rule or two to make the magic.

Being a Soloist.

Look at your competition. Look at what they are doing and don't do that. You'd don't want your home to look and feel like everyone else's. You don't want your RAL brand of homes to be confused with that of others. So think of a different approach, a different idea for a logo. We will go into the various kinds of logos later.

Symmetry.

There is a sacred geometry on earth and everything is inside of this equation. Even if we are not consciously aware of it, we humans do seek out symmetry. We find beauty in symmetry. We find health in symmetry. So symmetry can be very powerful in a Logo. When you are creating your Logo, make sure that there is a mathematical symmetry to every element inside the design.

Story.

Every one of your branding landmarks is an element to extend your brand stories. So, it started with the name, extended with the tagline, and now we're at the logo. Is the logo congruent with the emotional promise inside the name and inside the tagline? Are you giving the same exact emotional experience every time? Because people are counting on you to do that.

Your target individuals are counting on you to provide a community where their expectations are met. That's why they come and live in your home. Remember how powerful the flag is? Emblems are things that we live and die for. That we fight to protect. Your logo really becomes the symbol of your values and ethics, and the greater future inside your home.

So, for the 5 S's of not sucking: keep it simple, get them to take a second look, be a soloist, don't be like everyone else, employ the magic and mastery of symmetry, and always tell a compelling story.

Visual Storytelling Using the 3 Types of Logos

Visual storytelling is the most ancient form of getting ideas across. It's who we are as humans. We are visual creatures and your visual branding is projecting your story. What is the story that you want to tell? What are the images that belong inside of your brand? What are the images that don't?

The architecture of your brand will determine the emotional flow of each individual that enters your brand. Architecture is very subtle, but so very powerful at the same time. So, ask yourself: What images are on brand for you and what images are off brand for you? Tell your story eloquently and make it feel like a curated, beautiful, artistic expression of your visual story.

What are the three types of logos that you can create for your brand?

1. **The image based logo.** An image that can stand on its own and represent your brand. For example, the Lacoste Crocodiles, the Apple logo, the target symbol.

You see such logos and recognize the brand without seeing the name.

2. **The word based logo.** Solely the word, like Google or Disney or Coca-Cola. It's the letters themselves, and the font and the color that become the Logo of the brand.

3. **The image and word combination logo.** This would be something like Little Caesars, or Domino's Pizza, or even McDonalds.

Your RAL home brand can have a logo that is an image, words standing alone or a combination of the two. Pretty straightforward.

What is the takeaway?: The Dos And Don'ts Of Logos

Your logo needs to promise comfort and care, company and compassion. Your target individuals should want to call your home their home, and joyfully so. They need to feel loved and welcome. You can evoke all these emotions through your logo. Let's go over the dos and don'ts of creating a logo that works for you.

- Don't do what your competition is doing.
  - Do make your logo stand out from the rest.
- Don't try to make your logo about a lot of things.
  - Do convey a clear emotion.
- Don't underestimate the power of your logo.
  - Do use it to further the promise made by your name and tagline.

Glossary

Advertising - A marketing technique used to promote your brand, product, service, promotion, or other component of your business.

Algorithm - A process for analyzing reports and making problem-solving decisions based on the report data.

Back Up - Using a hard drive or other service to backup and save your information in case of computer errors, viruses, and crashes.

Compress - Compress files and images into smaller sizes for better web access and display. Some wordpress plugins will automatically compress your files and images when you upload them. This is vital for faster web page load times.

Domain - Your domain is your website. For google, there domain is google.com. However, this is not to be confused with a URL.

Geolocate, Geolocation - Locating people geographically so to be able to target these individuals based on their location. This helps your business when you do targeted advertising, as well as displaying your information to potential consumers that are local to your business.

Geotag - Tagging something with its geographic location. For instance, someone may create a Facebook post that tags their location or business they are at during the time of creating that post. This is a great way for users to find you and for you to promote your house, especially since your advantage is having a location in your URL.

Google My Business (GMB) - A free business service provided by Google. This service allows you to post, edit, and monitor your business listing and information. GMB is also a great way to gather and analyze your analytic reports.

Google Search Algorithm - Google uses an algorithm to rank businesses and websites based on consistency, social engagement, reviews, activity, and the content on your website. If you are consistent and relevant, your website will be higher ranked. However, inconsistencies and being to salesy in content will cause Google to derank you in the search results.

Ideal Individuals - Your ideal individuals are also known as your target audience and consumers or customers. These are the people you build your website and business around. For you, your ideal individuals consist of the children who will be putting their parents into your home.

Land Grab/ Land Run - A large scale land acquisition, as seen with the settling in the Wild West. In association with this book, the Land Grab applies to your need to get your URL before someone else snatches it up.

Marketing - The process of finding, creating, maintaining, and promoting relationships with your ideal individuals.

Pay Per Click (PPC) - An advertisement technique that can become very expensive as the advertiser pays for every click through the link. However, this is not very targeted so for local businesses this technique is not as beneficial as other advertisement techniques.

Portable Document Format (PDF) - A document that is formatted to work on multiple computer systems for a more cohesive way to share viewable documents to everyone.

Promoting/Promotion - Using a variety of marketing techniques to get your business name out to your ideal individuals.

Residential Assisted Living (RAL) - Senior care in a residential setting. The name for this may vary based on your state. It may be known as "Assisted Living" or other.

Resolution - This is the amount of detail a product has. For instance, higher resolution images are of better and crisper quality than lower resolution images. The same is applied to videos.

Responsive Website - A website that adjusts and renders web content based on the size of the screen the website is being viewed on. This is also known as being mobile friendly.

Search Engine - A website designed to allow users to search the World Wide Web for information.

Search Engine Optimization (SEO) - Using multiple tools and

techniques to adjust online and search engine presence and visibility. This is shown commonly in the use of interest specific keywords in web pages, in the name, in the tagline, and wherever else they can be used.

Search Frequency Data - Information that you can gain from your analytic reports. This information will give you insight into the trends in your search results and activity.

Social Engagement - Being involved in the online community through social media platforms and various websites. This also includes how your consumers respond to your business and content through actions such as likes, comments, and shares.

Social Media - Platforms that allow users to communicate and interact with each other. These platforms are vital for promoting your business to your ideal individuals.

Stock Images - High quality images that are either free or purchased for use on your website and print materials. While these may be a great resource for the right circumstances, it is important that you provide high quality non-stock images of your home and staff on your website and social media pages.

Tagline - A company catch phrase that is short, simple, adds to the story of your name and tugs on the emotion strings of your ideal individuals.

Target Audience - your ideal individuals are the audience that you will target your marketing, content, and website towards.

Top-Level Domain (TDL) - The ending of your domain name. These are known as .com, .net, .org, .biz, .info, .edu, etc.

Uniform Resource Locator (URL) - The web address to a page on a website. Multiple URLs may point to the same website, but different pages on that website. For instance, a website with an about and staff page will be housed on the same domain but have their own unique URLs.

Web Hosting - A service that hosts or stores your website on the World Wide Web. In order for your domain/website to be listed on the Internet, it has to be stored by a Web Hosting Provider.

Made in the USA
San Bernardino, CA
27 February 2019